50 Croissants to Danish Recipes

By: Kelly Johnson

Table of Contents

- Classic Butter Croissants
- Almond Croissants
- Chocolate Croissants
- Ham and Cheese Croissants
- Spinach and Feta Croissants
- Raspberry Jam Croissants
- Pistachio Croissants
- Apricot Croissants
- Cinnamon Sugar Croissants
- Blueberry Croissants
- Croissant Bread Pudding
- Lemon Cream Cheese Croissants
- Apple Cinnamon Danish
- Danish Pastry with Custard
- Cherry Danish
- Almond Cream Danish
- Raspberry Danish
- Chocolate Hazelnut Danish
- Pear and Almond Danish
- Danish Pastry with Cream Cheese
- Maple Pecan Croissants
- Banana Nut Croissants
- Peach Danish
- Nutella Croissants
- Orange Marmalade Danish
- Mocha Almond Croissants
- Egg and Cheese Croissants
- Poppy Seed Danish
- Strawberry Cream Cheese Croissants
- Vanilla Cream Danish
- Caramel Apple Danish
- Coconut Cream Danish
- Cinnamon Roll Croissants
- Pumpkin Spice Croissants
- Cranberry Almond Danish

- Blueberry Cream Cheese Danish
- Fig and Walnut Croissants
- Savory Ham and Gruyère Croissants
- Bacon, Egg, and Cheese Croissants
- Lemon Poppy Seed Danish
- Cranberry Orange Croissants
- Caramelized Onion and Goat Cheese Croissants
- Chocolate Mint Croissants
- Ginger Pear Danish
- Lemon Raspberry Danish
- Spiced Plum Danish
- Churro Croissants
- Apple and Brie Croissants
- Smoked Salmon and Cream Cheese Croissants
- Meringue-Topped Danish

Classic Butter Croissants
Ingredients:

- 4 cups all-purpose flour
- 1/2 cup water
- 1/2 cup whole milk
- 1/4 cup sugar
- 1 tbsp active dry yeast
- 2 tsp salt
- 1/2 cup unsalted butter, softened
- 2 sticks unsalted butter, cold
- 1 egg, for egg wash

Instructions:

1. In a bowl, combine water, milk, sugar, and yeast. Let it sit for 5 minutes to activate.
2. Add flour and salt to the yeast mixture and stir until a dough forms. Knead for 8-10 minutes until smooth.
3. Shape the dough into a ball and let it rise in a covered bowl for 1-2 hours, or until doubled in size.
4. Roll the dough out into a rectangle and place the cold butter in the center. Fold the dough over to enclose the butter.
5. Roll out the dough into a large rectangle, fold into thirds, and refrigerate for 30 minutes. Repeat this folding process 3 more times.
6. Roll the dough out again and cut into triangles. Roll up each triangle tightly to form croissants.
7. Let the croissants rise for about 1 hour, then brush with egg wash.
8. Preheat the oven to 375°F (190°C) and bake for 15-20 minutes or until golden and puffed.
9. Serve warm.

Almond Croissants
Ingredients:

- 6 classic butter croissants (day-old croissants work best)
- 1/2 cup almond paste
- 1/4 cup powdered sugar
- 2 tbsp unsalted butter, softened
- 1 egg
- 1/2 tsp almond extract
- Sliced almonds for topping
- Powdered sugar for dusting

Instructions:

1. Slice the croissants in half horizontally.
2. In a bowl, mix almond paste, powdered sugar, softened butter, egg, and almond extract until smooth.
3. Spread the almond mixture on the bottom halves of the croissants and close them back up.
4. Preheat the oven to 350°F (175°C). Place the filled croissants on a baking sheet.
5. Brush the tops with a little egg wash and sprinkle with sliced almonds.
6. Bake for 10-12 minutes, or until golden brown.
7. Dust with powdered sugar before serving.

Chocolate Croissants
Ingredients:

- 6 classic butter croissants
- 1/2 cup semisweet chocolate chips or chocolate bars (chopped)
- 1 egg (for egg wash)

Instructions:

1. Slice the croissants in half horizontally.
2. Place a tablespoon of chocolate chips or chopped chocolate inside each croissant.
3. Close the croissants and brush with egg wash.
4. Preheat the oven to 375°F (190°C). Place the croissants on a baking sheet.
5. Bake for 12-15 minutes, or until the croissants are golden brown and the chocolate has melted.
6. Serve warm.

Ham and Cheese Croissants
Ingredients:

- 6 classic butter croissants
- 6 slices deli ham
- 6 slices Swiss cheese
- 1 egg (for egg wash)

Instructions:

1. Slice the croissants in half horizontally.
2. Place a slice of ham and a slice of Swiss cheese inside each croissant.
3. Close the croissants and brush the tops with egg wash.
4. Preheat the oven to 375°F (190°C). Place the croissants on a baking sheet.
5. Bake for 10-12 minutes, or until the croissants are golden brown and the cheese is melted.
6. Serve warm.

Spinach and Feta Croissants

Ingredients:

- 6 classic butter croissants
- 1 cup cooked spinach, squeezed dry
- 1/2 cup crumbled feta cheese
- 1/4 cup ricotta cheese
- 1 egg (for egg wash)

Instructions:

1. Slice the croissants in half horizontally.
2. In a bowl, mix cooked spinach, feta cheese, and ricotta cheese.
3. Spoon the spinach mixture inside each croissant and close them back up.
4. Brush the croissants with egg wash.
5. Preheat the oven to 375°F (190°C). Place the croissants on a baking sheet.
6. Bake for 12-15 minutes, or until golden and crisp.
7. Serve warm.

Raspberry Jam Croissants
Ingredients:

- 6 classic butter croissants
- 1/4 cup raspberry jam or preserves
- Powdered sugar for dusting

Instructions:

1. Slice the croissants in half horizontally.
2. Spread a tablespoon of raspberry jam on the inside of each croissant.
3. Close the croissants and bake at 375°F (190°C) for 10-12 minutes, or until golden.
4. Dust with powdered sugar before serving.

Pistachio Croissants
Ingredients:

- 6 classic butter croissants
- 1/2 cup shelled pistachios, finely chopped
- 1/4 cup powdered sugar
- 2 tbsp unsalted butter, softened
- 1/4 tsp vanilla extract
- 1 egg (for egg wash)

Instructions:

1. Slice the croissants in half horizontally.
2. In a bowl, combine pistachios, powdered sugar, softened butter, and vanilla extract.
3. Spread the pistachio mixture inside the croissants.
4. Close the croissants and brush with egg wash.
5. Preheat the oven to 375°F (190°C). Place the croissants on a baking sheet.
6. Bake for 12-15 minutes, or until golden and crisp.
7. Serve warm.

Apricot Croissants
Ingredients:

- 6 classic butter croissants
- 1/4 cup apricot jam or preserves
- 1/4 cup chopped dried apricots
- Powdered sugar for dusting

Instructions:

1. Slice the croissants in half horizontally.
2. Spread apricot jam inside each croissant and sprinkle with chopped dried apricots.
3. Close the croissants and bake at 375°F (190°C) for 10-12 minutes, or until golden.
4. Dust with powdered sugar before serving.

These croissant variations provide a delightful array of sweet and savory options for any breakfast or brunch gathering!

Cinnamon Sugar Croissants
Ingredients:

- 6 classic butter croissants
- 1/4 cup granulated sugar
- 1 tbsp ground cinnamon
- 2 tbsp unsalted butter, melted

Instructions:

1. Preheat the oven to 375°F (190°C).
2. Slice the croissants in half horizontally or leave whole depending on your preference.
3. In a small bowl, mix together the sugar and cinnamon.
4. Brush the croissants with melted butter and sprinkle the cinnamon sugar mixture generously over them.
5. Bake for 10-12 minutes, or until golden and crisp.
6. Serve warm, optionally dusted with extra powdered sugar.

Blueberry Croissants
Ingredients:

- 6 classic butter croissants
- 1/2 cup fresh blueberries
- 2 tbsp sugar
- 1/2 cup mascarpone cheese
- 1 egg (for egg wash)

Instructions:

1. Preheat the oven to 375°F (190°C).
2. Slice the croissants in half horizontally.
3. In a small bowl, combine the mascarpone cheese and sugar. Spread this mixture inside each croissant.
4. Fill each croissant with fresh blueberries.
5. Close the croissants and brush the tops with egg wash.
6. Bake for 12-15 minutes, until golden and the cheese has melted.
7. Serve warm.

Croissant Bread Pudding
Ingredients:

- 6 classic butter croissants, torn into pieces
- 2 cups whole milk
- 1/2 cup heavy cream
- 3/4 cup granulated sugar
- 4 large eggs
- 1 tbsp vanilla extract
- 1/2 tsp ground cinnamon
- 1/2 cup raisins or dried fruit (optional)
- Powdered sugar for dusting

Instructions:

1. Preheat the oven to 350°F (175°C) and butter a baking dish.
2. Tear the croissants into pieces and place them in the baking dish.
3. In a bowl, whisk together milk, cream, sugar, eggs, vanilla, and cinnamon. Pour over the croissant pieces, pressing them down gently to soak the mixture.
4. Let the bread pudding sit for 10-15 minutes to absorb the liquid, then scatter raisins if using.
5. Bake for 30-35 minutes, or until set and golden.
6. Dust with powdered sugar and serve warm with whipped cream or vanilla ice cream.

Lemon Cream Cheese Croissants
Ingredients:

- 6 classic butter croissants
- 1/2 cup cream cheese, softened
- 1/4 cup powdered sugar
- 1 tbsp lemon juice
- 1 tsp lemon zest
- 1 egg (for egg wash)

Instructions:

1. Preheat the oven to 375°F (190°C).
2. Slice the croissants in half horizontally.
3. In a bowl, mix together the cream cheese, powdered sugar, lemon juice, and zest until smooth.
4. Spread the lemon cream cheese mixture inside each croissant and close them up.
5. Brush the tops with egg wash.
6. Bake for 10-12 minutes, or until golden.
7. Serve warm, optionally garnished with extra lemon zest.

Apple Cinnamon Danish
Ingredients:

- 6 classic butter croissants
- 1 large apple, peeled and diced
- 1/4 cup granulated sugar
- 1 tsp ground cinnamon
- 2 tbsp unsalted butter
- 1/2 cup cream cheese, softened
- 1/4 cup powdered sugar

Instructions:

1. Preheat the oven to 375°F (190°C).
2. Slice the croissants in half horizontally and set aside.
3. In a small skillet, melt butter over medium heat. Add the diced apple, sugar, and cinnamon, and cook for 5-7 minutes until softened and caramelized.
4. Spread the apple mixture inside each croissant.
5. In a separate bowl, mix cream cheese and powdered sugar to create a glaze.
6. Bake the croissants for 10-12 minutes, or until golden. Drizzle with the cream cheese glaze before serving.

Danish Pastry with Custard
Ingredients:

- 6 classic butter croissants
- 1/2 cup pastry cream (store-bought or homemade)
- 1 egg (for egg wash)

Instructions:

1. Preheat the oven to 375°F (190°C).
2. Slice the croissants in half horizontally.
3. Fill each croissant with a generous spoonful of pastry cream.
4. Brush the croissants with egg wash.
5. Bake for 10-12 minutes, or until the croissants are golden and the pastry cream is set.
6. Serve warm, optionally topped with a dusting of powdered sugar.

Cherry Danish
Ingredients:

- 6 classic butter croissants
- 1/2 cup cherry preserves or fresh cherries
- 2 tbsp cream cheese, softened
- 1/4 tsp vanilla extract
- 1 egg (for egg wash)

Instructions:

1. Preheat the oven to 375°F (190°C).
2. Slice the croissants in half horizontally.
3. In a bowl, mix the cream cheese and vanilla extract. Spread this mixture inside each croissant.
4. Top with a spoonful of cherry preserves or fresh cherries.
5. Close the croissants and brush with egg wash.
6. Bake for 10-12 minutes, or until golden and puffed.
7. Serve warm.

Almond Cream Danish
Ingredients:

- 6 classic butter croissants
- 1/2 cup almond paste
- 1/4 cup powdered sugar
- 2 tbsp unsalted butter, softened
- 1 egg (for egg wash)
- Sliced almonds for garnish

Instructions:

1. Preheat the oven to 375°F (190°C).
2. Slice the croissants in half horizontally.
3. In a bowl, mix almond paste, powdered sugar, and softened butter. Spread this mixture inside each croissant.
4. Close the croissants and brush with egg wash.
5. Sprinkle with sliced almonds.
6. Bake for 10-12 minutes, or until golden.
7. Serve warm.

Raspberry Danish
Ingredients:

- 6 classic butter croissants
- 1/2 cup raspberry jam or fresh raspberries
- 2 tbsp cream cheese, softened
- 2 tbsp powdered sugar
- 1 egg (for egg wash)

Instructions:

1. Preheat the oven to 375°F (190°C).
2. Slice the croissants in half horizontally.
3. In a small bowl, mix cream cheese and powdered sugar until smooth.
4. Spread the cream cheese mixture inside each croissant.
5. Add a spoonful of raspberry jam or fresh raspberries on top.
6. Close the croissants and brush with egg wash.
7. Bake for 10-12 minutes, or until golden and puffed.
8. Serve warm, optionally topped with extra powdered sugar.

Chocolate Hazelnut Danish
Ingredients:

- 6 classic butter croissants
- 1/4 cup hazelnut chocolate spread (such as Nutella)
- 1 tbsp chopped hazelnuts
- 1 egg (for egg wash)

Instructions:

1. Preheat the oven to 375°F (190°C).
2. Slice the croissants in half horizontally.
3. Spread a generous amount of hazelnut chocolate spread inside each croissant.
4. Sprinkle with chopped hazelnuts.
5. Close the croissants and brush with egg wash.
6. Bake for 10-12 minutes, or until golden and flaky.
7. Serve warm.

Pear and Almond Danish
Ingredients:

- 6 classic butter croissants
- 1 ripe pear, peeled and sliced
- 2 tbsp almond paste
- 1/4 cup sliced almonds
- 1 egg (for egg wash)

Instructions:

1. Preheat the oven to 375°F (190°C).
2. Slice the croissants in half horizontally.
3. In a small bowl, crumble almond paste and spread it inside each croissant.
4. Add a few slices of pear on top of the almond paste.
5. Sprinkle with sliced almonds.
6. Close the croissants and brush with egg wash.
7. Bake for 10-12 minutes, or until golden.
8. Serve warm.

Danish Pastry with Cream Cheese
Ingredients:

- 6 classic butter croissants
- 1/2 cup cream cheese, softened
- 2 tbsp powdered sugar
- 1 tsp vanilla extract
- 1 egg (for egg wash)

Instructions:

1. Preheat the oven to 375°F (190°C).
2. Slice the croissants in half horizontally.
3. In a bowl, combine cream cheese, powdered sugar, and vanilla extract.
4. Spread the cream cheese mixture inside each croissant.
5. Close the croissants and brush with egg wash.
6. Bake for 10-12 minutes, or until golden.
7. Serve warm.

Maple Pecan Croissants
Ingredients:

- 6 classic butter croissants
- 1/4 cup maple syrup
- 1/2 cup chopped pecans
- 2 tbsp butter, melted
- 1 egg (for egg wash)

Instructions:

1. Preheat the oven to 375°F (190°C).
2. Slice the croissants in half horizontally.
3. Brush the inside of each croissant with melted butter.
4. Drizzle with maple syrup and sprinkle with chopped pecans.
5. Close the croissants and brush with egg wash.
6. Bake for 10-12 minutes, or until golden and crisp.
7. Serve warm.

Banana Nut Croissants
Ingredients:

- 6 classic butter croissants
- 1 ripe banana, mashed
- 1/4 cup chopped walnuts or pecans
- 2 tbsp honey
- 1 egg (for egg wash)

Instructions:

1. Preheat the oven to 375°F (190°C).
2. Slice the croissants in half horizontally.
3. Mash the banana in a small bowl and spread it inside each croissant.
4. Sprinkle with chopped nuts and drizzle with honey.
5. Close the croissants and brush with egg wash.
6. Bake for 10-12 minutes, or until golden.
7. Serve warm.

Peach Danish
Ingredients:

- 6 classic butter croissants
- 1/2 cup peach preserves or fresh peaches, sliced
- 2 tbsp cream cheese, softened
- 1 tbsp honey
- 1 egg (for egg wash)

Instructions:

1. Preheat the oven to 375°F (190°C).
2. Slice the croissants in half horizontally.
3. Spread cream cheese on the inside of each croissant.
4. Add a spoonful of peach preserves or fresh peach slices on top.
5. Drizzle with honey.
6. Close the croissants and brush with egg wash.
7. Bake for 10-12 minutes, or until golden and puffy.
8. Serve warm.

Nutella Croissants
Ingredients:

- 6 classic butter croissants
- 1/4 cup Nutella or other hazelnut chocolate spread
- 1 egg (for egg wash)

Instructions:

1. Preheat the oven to 375°F (190°C).
2. Slice the croissants in half horizontally.
3. Spread a generous amount of Nutella inside each croissant.
4. Close the croissants and brush with egg wash.
5. Bake for 10-12 minutes, or until golden and flaky.
6. Serve warm.

Orange Marmalade Danish
Ingredients:

- 6 classic butter croissants
- 1/4 cup orange marmalade
- 2 tbsp cream cheese, softened
- 1 egg (for egg wash)

Instructions:

1. Preheat the oven to 375°F (190°C).
2. Slice the croissants in half horizontally.
3. Spread a thin layer of cream cheese inside each croissant.
4. Add a spoonful of orange marmalade on top.
5. Close the croissants and brush with egg wash.
6. Bake for 10-12 minutes, or until golden and puffed.
7. Serve warm.

Mocha Almond Croissants
Ingredients:

- 6 classic butter croissants
- 1/4 cup chocolate hazelnut spread (e.g., Nutella)
- 1 tbsp instant coffee or espresso powder
- 1/4 cup sliced almonds
- 1 egg (for egg wash)

Instructions:

1. Preheat the oven to 375°F (190°C).
2. Slice the croissants in half horizontally.
3. In a small bowl, mix the chocolate spread and instant coffee until smooth.
4. Spread the mocha chocolate mixture inside each croissant.
5. Sprinkle with sliced almonds.
6. Close the croissants and brush with egg wash.
7. Bake for 10-12 minutes, or until golden and crispy.
8. Serve warm.

Egg and Cheese Croissants

Ingredients:

- 6 classic butter croissants
- 4 large eggs, scrambled
- 1/2 cup shredded cheddar cheese
- Salt and pepper to taste
- 1 egg (for egg wash)

Instructions:

1. Preheat the oven to 375°F (190°C).
2. Slice the croissants in half horizontally.
3. Scramble the eggs in a pan, adding salt and pepper to taste.
4. Place a spoonful of scrambled eggs inside each croissant and top with shredded cheddar cheese.
5. Close the croissants and brush with egg wash.
6. Bake for 10-12 minutes, or until golden.
7. Serve warm.

Poppy Seed Danish
Ingredients:

- 6 classic butter croissants
- 1/4 cup poppy seeds
- 1/4 cup cream cheese, softened
- 2 tbsp powdered sugar
- 1 egg (for egg wash)

Instructions:

1. Preheat the oven to 375°F (190°C).
2. Slice the croissants in half horizontally.
3. In a small bowl, combine cream cheese and powdered sugar.
4. Spread the cream cheese mixture inside each croissant.
5. Sprinkle with poppy seeds.
6. Close the croissants and brush with egg wash.
7. Bake for 10-12 minutes, or until golden and puffed.
8. Serve warm.

Strawberry Cream Cheese Croissants
Ingredients:

- 6 classic butter croissants
- 1/4 cup cream cheese, softened
- 2 tbsp powdered sugar
- 1/4 cup strawberry jam or fresh strawberries, chopped
- 1 egg (for egg wash)

Instructions:

1. Preheat the oven to 375°F (190°C).
2. Slice the croissants in half horizontally.
3. In a small bowl, mix cream cheese and powdered sugar until smooth.
4. Spread the cream cheese mixture inside each croissant.
5. Add a spoonful of strawberry jam or fresh strawberries on top.
6. Close the croissants and brush with egg wash.
7. Bake for 10-12 minutes, or until golden and puffy.
8. Serve warm.

Vanilla Cream Danish

Ingredients:

- 6 classic butter croissants
- 1/4 cup vanilla custard or vanilla pudding
- 1/2 tsp vanilla extract
- 2 tbsp sliced almonds
- 1 egg (for egg wash)

Instructions:

1. Preheat the oven to 375°F (190°C).
2. Slice the croissants in half horizontally.
3. In a bowl, combine vanilla custard and vanilla extract.
4. Spread the vanilla cream inside each croissant.
5. Sprinkle with sliced almonds.
6. Close the croissants and brush with egg wash.
7. Bake for 10-12 minutes, or until golden and crispy.
8. Serve warm.

Caramel Apple Danish
Ingredients:

- 6 classic butter croissants
- 1 medium apple, peeled and sliced
- 1/4 cup caramel sauce
- 2 tbsp cream cheese, softened
- 1 egg (for egg wash)

Instructions:

1. Preheat the oven to 375°F (190°C).
2. Slice the croissants in half horizontally.
3. In a small bowl, mix cream cheese and caramel sauce.
4. Spread the mixture inside each croissant.
5. Add a few slices of apple on top of the caramel mixture.
6. Close the croissants and brush with egg wash.
7. Bake for 10-12 minutes, or until golden.
8. Serve warm.

Coconut Cream Danish
Ingredients:

- 6 classic butter croissants
- 1/4 cup shredded coconut
- 1/4 cup cream cheese, softened
- 2 tbsp powdered sugar
- 1 tsp coconut extract
- 1 egg (for egg wash)

Instructions:

1. Preheat the oven to 375°F (190°C).
2. Slice the croissants in half horizontally.
3. In a small bowl, combine cream cheese, powdered sugar, and coconut extract.
4. Spread the coconut cream mixture inside each croissant.
5. Sprinkle with shredded coconut.
6. Close the croissants and brush with egg wash.
7. Bake for 10-12 minutes, or until golden and puffy.
8. Serve warm.

Cinnamon Roll Croissants
Ingredients:

- 6 classic butter croissants
- 1/4 cup butter, melted
- 1/4 cup brown sugar
- 1 tbsp ground cinnamon
- 1/4 cup cream cheese, softened
- 1 tbsp powdered sugar
- 1 tsp vanilla extract
- 1 egg (for egg wash)

Instructions:

1. Preheat the oven to 375°F (190°C).
2. Slice the croissants in half horizontally.
3. In a small bowl, mix melted butter, brown sugar, and cinnamon.
4. Spread the cinnamon mixture inside each croissant.
5. Close the croissants and brush with egg wash.
6. In another small bowl, mix cream cheese, powdered sugar, and vanilla extract to make the glaze.
7. Bake croissants for 10-12 minutes, or until golden and puffed.
8. Drizzle with the cream cheese glaze before serving.

Pumpkin Spice Croissants
Ingredients:

- 6 classic butter croissants
- 1/4 cup canned pumpkin puree
- 2 tbsp brown sugar
- 1 tsp pumpkin pie spice
- 1/4 cup cream cheese, softened
- 1 tsp vanilla extract
- 1 egg (for egg wash)

Instructions:

1. Preheat the oven to 375°F (190°C).
2. Slice the croissants in half horizontally.
3. In a small bowl, mix pumpkin puree, brown sugar, and pumpkin pie spice.
4. Spread the pumpkin mixture inside each croissant.
5. Close the croissants and brush with egg wash.
6. In another small bowl, mix cream cheese and vanilla extract.
7. Bake for 10-12 minutes, or until golden and puffed.
8. Serve warm with a dollop of cream cheese mixture.

Cranberry Almond Danish
Ingredients:

- 6 classic butter croissants
- 1/4 cup cranberry sauce or fresh cranberries
- 1/4 cup sliced almonds
- 1/4 cup cream cheese, softened
- 2 tbsp honey
- 1 egg (for egg wash)

Instructions:

1. Preheat the oven to 375°F (190°C).
2. Slice the croissants in half horizontally.
3. Spread a thin layer of cream cheese inside each croissant.
4. Add a spoonful of cranberry sauce or fresh cranberries on top.
5. Sprinkle with sliced almonds and drizzle with honey.
6. Close the croissants and brush with egg wash.
7. Bake for 10-12 minutes, or until golden and puffed.
8. Serve warm.

Blueberry Cream Cheese Danish
Ingredients:

- 6 classic butter croissants
- 1/4 cup cream cheese, softened
- 2 tbsp powdered sugar
- 1/2 cup fresh blueberries
- 1 tsp vanilla extract
- 1 egg (for egg wash)

Instructions:

1. Preheat the oven to 375°F (190°C).
2. Slice the croissants in half horizontally.
3. In a small bowl, mix cream cheese, powdered sugar, and vanilla extract.
4. Spread the cream cheese mixture inside each croissant.
5. Add fresh blueberries on top of the cream cheese.
6. Close the croissants and brush with egg wash.
7. Bake for 10-12 minutes, or until golden and puffed.
8. Serve warm.

Fig and Walnut Croissants
Ingredients:

- 6 classic butter croissants
- 1/4 cup dried figs, chopped
- 1/4 cup walnuts, chopped
- 1/4 cup honey
- 1/4 cup cream cheese, softened
- 1 egg (for egg wash)

Instructions:

1. Preheat the oven to 375°F (190°C).
2. Slice the croissants in half horizontally.
3. In a small bowl, mix chopped figs, walnuts, and honey.
4. Spread a layer of cream cheese inside each croissant.
5. Add the fig and walnut mixture on top.
6. Close the croissants and brush with egg wash.
7. Bake for 10-12 minutes, or until golden and puffed.
8. Serve warm.

Savory Ham and Gruyère Croissants

Ingredients:

- 6 classic butter croissants
- 1/2 cup ham, thinly sliced
- 1/2 cup Gruyère cheese, shredded
- 1 egg (for egg wash)
- Fresh thyme (optional)

Instructions:

1. Preheat the oven to 375°F (190°C).
2. Slice the croissants in half horizontally.
3. Layer the ham and Gruyère cheese inside each croissant.
4. Add a sprinkle of fresh thyme (optional).
5. Close the croissants and brush with egg wash.
6. Bake for 10-12 minutes, or until golden and the cheese is melted.
7. Serve warm.

Bacon, Egg, and Cheese Croissants
Ingredients:

- 6 classic butter croissants
- 4 large eggs, scrambled
- 1/2 cup cooked bacon, crumbled
- 1/2 cup shredded cheddar cheese
- Salt and pepper to taste
- 1 egg (for egg wash)

Instructions:

1. Preheat the oven to 375°F (190°C).
2. Slice the croissants in half horizontally.
3. Scramble the eggs in a pan, adding salt and pepper to taste.
4. Layer scrambled eggs, crumbled bacon, and shredded cheddar cheese inside each croissant.
5. Close the croissants and brush with egg wash.
6. Bake for 10-12 minutes, or until golden and cheese is melted.
7. Serve warm.

Lemon Poppy Seed Danish
Ingredients:

- 6 classic butter croissants
- 1/4 cup cream cheese, softened
- 2 tbsp powdered sugar
- 1 tsp lemon zest
- 1 tbsp poppy seeds
- 1 egg (for egg wash)

Instructions:

1. Preheat the oven to 375°F (190°C).
2. Slice the croissants in half horizontally.
3. In a small bowl, mix cream cheese, powdered sugar, lemon zest, and poppy seeds.
4. Spread the lemon cream cheese mixture inside each croissant.
5. Close the croissants and brush with egg wash.
6. Bake for 10-12 minutes, or until golden and puffed.
7. Serve warm.

Cranberry Orange Croissants
Ingredients:

- 6 classic butter croissants
- 1/2 cup fresh cranberries, chopped
- 1/4 cup orange zest
- 1/4 cup powdered sugar
- 1/4 cup cream cheese, softened
- 1 egg (for egg wash)

Instructions:

1. Preheat the oven to 375°F (190°C).
2. Slice the croissants in half horizontally.
3. In a small bowl, mix cranberries, orange zest, and powdered sugar.
4. Spread a thin layer of cream cheese inside each croissant.
5. Add the cranberry-orange mixture on top.
6. Close the croissants and brush with egg wash.
7. Bake for 10-12 minutes, or until golden and puffed.
8. Serve warm.

Caramelized Onion and Goat Cheese Croissants
Ingredients:

- 6 classic butter croissants
- 1/2 cup caramelized onions
- 1/4 cup goat cheese, crumbled
- Fresh thyme leaves (optional)
- 1 egg (for egg wash)

Instructions:

1. Preheat the oven to 375°F (190°C).
2. Slice the croissants in half horizontally.
3. Spread a thin layer of goat cheese inside each croissant.
4. Top with caramelized onions and fresh thyme (if desired).
5. Close the croissants and brush with egg wash.
6. Bake for 10-12 minutes, or until golden and the cheese is melted.
7. Serve warm.

Chocolate Mint Croissants
Ingredients:

- 6 classic butter croissants
- 1/4 cup semisweet chocolate chips
- 1/4 cup fresh mint leaves, chopped
- 1 tbsp powdered sugar (for dusting)
- 1 egg (for egg wash)

Instructions:

1. Preheat the oven to 375°F (190°C).
2. Slice the croissants in half horizontally.
3. Sprinkle chocolate chips and chopped mint leaves inside each croissant.
4. Close the croissants and brush with egg wash.
5. Bake for 10-12 minutes, or until golden and the chocolate has melted.
6. Dust with powdered sugar before serving.

Ginger Pear Danish
Ingredients:

- 6 classic butter croissants
- 1 pear, peeled and diced
- 1/4 cup sugar
- 1/2 tsp ground ginger
- 1/4 cup cream cheese, softened
- 1 tsp vanilla extract
- 1 egg (for egg wash)

Instructions:

1. Preheat the oven to 375°F (190°C).
2. Slice the croissants in half horizontally.
3. In a small saucepan, heat diced pear, sugar, and ginger over medium heat until soft and caramelized, about 5 minutes.
4. In a separate bowl, mix cream cheese and vanilla extract.
5. Spread cream cheese inside each croissant, then top with the ginger-pear mixture.
6. Close the croissants and brush with egg wash.
7. Bake for 10-12 minutes, or until golden and puffed.
8. Serve warm.

Lemon Raspberry Danish
Ingredients:

- 6 classic butter croissants
- 1/4 cup fresh raspberries
- 1 tbsp lemon zest
- 1/4 cup cream cheese, softened
- 2 tbsp powdered sugar
- 1 egg (for egg wash)

Instructions:

1. Preheat the oven to 375°F (190°C).
2. Slice the croissants in half horizontally.
3. In a small bowl, mix cream cheese, powdered sugar, and lemon zest.
4. Spread the cream cheese mixture inside each croissant.
5. Add a few raspberries on top of the cream cheese.
6. Close the croissants and brush with egg wash.
7. Bake for 10-12 minutes, or until golden and puffed.
8. Serve warm.

Spiced Plum Danish
Ingredients:

- 6 classic butter croissants
- 2 ripe plums, pitted and sliced
- 1 tbsp brown sugar
- 1/2 tsp cinnamon
- 1/4 tsp ground cloves
- 1/4 cup cream cheese, softened
- 1 tbsp honey
- 1 egg (for egg wash)

Instructions:

1. Preheat the oven to 375°F (190°C).
2. Slice the croissants in half horizontally.
3. In a bowl, combine sliced plums, brown sugar, cinnamon, and ground cloves. Let sit for 5 minutes.
4. Mix cream cheese with honey until smooth.
5. Spread the cream cheese mixture inside each croissant.
6. Top with the spiced plum mixture.
7. Close the croissants and brush with egg wash.
8. Bake for 10-12 minutes, or until golden and puffed.
9. Serve warm.

Churro Croissants
Ingredients:

- 6 classic butter croissants
- 1/2 cup sugar
- 1 tsp ground cinnamon
- 2 tbsp melted butter
- 1 egg (for egg wash)

Instructions:

1. Preheat the oven to 375°F (190°C).
2. Slice the croissants in half horizontally.
3. Brush each croissant with melted butter.
4. In a small bowl, mix sugar and cinnamon. Sprinkle generously over the buttered croissants.
5. Close the croissants and brush with egg wash.
6. Bake for 10-12 minutes, or until golden and crisp.
7. Serve warm.

Apple and Brie Croissants

Ingredients:

- 6 classic butter croissants
- 1 apple, thinly sliced
- 1/4 cup Brie cheese, sliced
- 1 tbsp honey
- 1/4 tsp ground cinnamon
- 1 egg (for egg wash)

Instructions:

1. Preheat the oven to 375°F (190°C).
2. Slice the croissants in half horizontally.
3. Layer the sliced apple and Brie cheese inside each croissant.
4. Drizzle with honey and sprinkle with cinnamon.
5. Close the croissants and brush with egg wash.
6. Bake for 10-12 minutes, or until golden and the cheese is melted.
7. Serve warm.

Smoked Salmon and Cream Cheese Croissants
Ingredients:

- 6 classic butter croissants
- 4 oz smoked salmon, thinly sliced
- 1/4 cup cream cheese, softened
- 1 tbsp fresh dill, chopped
- 1 tbsp capers (optional)
- 1 egg (for egg wash)

Instructions:

1. Preheat the oven to 375°F (190°C).
2. Slice the croissants in half horizontally.
3. Spread a generous layer of cream cheese inside each croissant.
4. Layer smoked salmon and sprinkle with fresh dill. Add capers if using.
5. Close the croissants and brush with egg wash.
6. Bake for 10-12 minutes, or until golden and puffed.
7. Serve warm.

Meringue-Topped Danish
Ingredients:

- 6 classic butter croissants
- 1/4 cup lemon curd or raspberry jam
- 2 egg whites
- 1/4 cup sugar
- 1/4 tsp vanilla extract
- 1 egg (for egg wash)

Instructions:

1. Preheat the oven to 375°F (190°C).
2. Slice the croissants in half horizontally.
3. Spread a thin layer of lemon curd or raspberry jam inside each croissant.
4. In a separate bowl, beat egg whites with sugar and vanilla extract until stiff peaks form.
5. Top each croissant with a generous spoonful of meringue.
6. Brush the edges of the croissants with egg wash.
7. Bake for 12-15 minutes, or until golden and the meringue is lightly browned.
8. Serve warm.